C000227120

THE LITTLE BOOK OF

CAKE DECORATING

TIPS

Meg Boas

THE LITTLE BOOK OF

CAKE DECORATING

TIPS

Meg Boas

A.

'All the world is birthday cake, so take a piece, but not too much.'

George Harrison

1. **When mixing coloured icing, make more than you need,** as it may be difficult to achieve exactly the same colour again.

"When mixing coloured icing, make more than you need."

2. To prevent crimping tools springing open and tearing your sugar paste, tie an elastic band around them.

"To prevent crimping tools springing open tie an elastic band around them.

3. **A quick** and easy **way to decorate a sponge cake is to place a paper doily on top** of the cake and shake icing sugar over it – take away the doily and you have an impressive pattern!

A quick way to decorate a sponge cake is to place a paper doily on top and shake icing sugar over it.

4.

Always **keep a separate wooden spoon especially for beating royal icing.** General-use spoons could be greasy and grease prevents egg whites expanding properly.

Keep a separate wooden spoon especially for beating royal icing.

5.

One way to **make your own embosser** is **by placing your design under a piece of Perspex** or glass, **and,** using a fine tube, **pipe royal icing around the outline of the drawing.** Once dry, lift the outline off the glass and press the design onto soft sugar paste.

"Make your own embosser
by placing your design under
a piece of Perspex and pipe
royal icing around the outline
of the drawing."

6. **Never try** and get away with **using soft margarine to make buttercream;** it won't taste good and will be too soft for piping.

"Never try using soft margarine to make buttercream."

7.

It's not always easy to cut a cake perfectly level just with an ordinary knife. To make it easier **invest in a cake leveller** and just set it to the desired height.

Invest in a cake leveller.

8. **To make** professional looking **sugar flowers, roll the flower paste very thinly** – so thin in fact, you could almost read through it.

"To make sugar flowers, roll the flower paste very thinly. "

9. **If your knife is sticking** to the buttercream whilst icing, don't panic, just **dip it occasionally into hot water,** dry, and then continue to use.

"If your knife is sticking dip
it occasionally into hot water."

10.

If you feel **daunted by the thought of writing freehand straight onto a cake,** use either an embosser, or special cutters or moulds to form letters out of sugar paste.

"Daunted by the thought of writing freehand straight onto a cake?"

11.

While working with royal icing, remember that sugar dries extremely quickly, so always **place a piece of dampened clingfilm or muslin over the bowl** to prevent it drying out.

"While working with royal icing, place a piece of dampened clingfilm or muslin over the bowl. "

12.

To **prevent** the **buttercream** in a piping bag **getting too warm** from your hands on a hot day, use a double thickness bag.

Prevent buttercream getting too warm.

13.

When making marzipan and sugar paste models for children's novelty cakes, **use raw dried spaghetti** instead of cocktail sticks to support their heads and limbs.

When making marzipan and sugar paste models use raw dried spaghetti to support their heads.

14.

Before slicing a cake into layers, make sure they can be replaced in their correct positions by cutting a small 'V' shape down the side of the cake. Use this 'V' as a guide when replacing the layers.

Before slicing a cake into layers...

15. To use ganache for piping, first refrigerate, and when firm, beat to a piping consistency.

"To use ganache for piping, refrigerate and beat to a piping consistency."

16.

Before placing a cake in a box, put a folded cloth or non-slip mat **onto the base of the box.** This will raise the cake slightly and make it easier to grip the cake board when lifting the cake from the box later.

"Before placing a cake in a box, put a folded cloth onto the base of the box.

17. Sugar paste does not like to get wet – moisture will dissolve the sugar leaving craters, so **keep all utensils clean and thoroughly dry.**

"Keep all utensils clean and thoroughly dry.

18. **For a glossier ganache, use double or whipping cream** rather than single; they both have a higher fat content which helps create the gloss.

"For a glossier ganache, use double or whipping cream."

19.

For creamier chocolatey buttercream with a lovely intense colour and taste, don't add the cocoa powder straight to the butter, instead, **dissolve the cocoa powder first in a little hot water** to form a paste and then add.

"For creamier chocolatey buttercream dissolve the cocoa powder first in a little hot water."

20.

Condensation can form on a chocolate cake taken straight from the freezer. To avoid this happening, **move the cake to the fridge to defrost the day before it's needed.**

"Move the cake to the fridge to defrost the day before it's needed."

21.

Paste food colours are better for colouring sugar pastes as opposed to liquid colours that can make the icing too sticky. But be warned, they **are surprisingly vibrant, so add very gradually** using a cocktail stick.

"Paste food colours are surprisingly vibrant, so add very gradually."

22.

Having trouble piping? Try brushing away mistakes with a damp paintbrush and try again.

"Having trouble piping?"

23.

If you would like an impressive looking 3-tier cake for a wedding, but two tiers will be sufficient cake for your guests, **consider using a dummy tier** for the third. They are widely available from cake decorating suppliers and can be decorated in just the same way as the other tiers. Just remember to tell the caterers!

"Consider using a dummy tier."

24. **Always use a metal ruler** (known as a straight edge) **to level the top of a royal iced cake;** a plastic one will bend under the weight of the icing and leave ridges.

Always use a metal ruler to level the top of a royal iced cake.

25.

Use two thin coats of buttercream, rather than one thick one, to achieve a truly smooth and even icing.

Use two thin coats of buttercream, rather than one thick one.

26. **To prevent getting into a sticky mess when making marzipan roses;** place the petals between two sheets of polythene and thin the petals through the surface.

"To prevent getting into a sticky mess when making marzipan roses...

27.

To make sugar roses look more real, always **make the centres a** slightly **deeper colour** than the outside petals.

"To make sugar roses look more real, make the centres a deeper colour."

28.

Before you pour icing over your fondant fancies, place a sheet of greaseproof **paper under the rack.** Any fondant that drips onto the paper below can be scraped off and reused.

"Before you pour icing over your fondant fancies, place paper under the rack."

29.

For complete accuracy, **always measure for a template after the cake has been iced** – not before. If taken directly from the cake surface the template will be too small.

Always measure for a template after the cake has been iced.

30.

To prevent sugar paste frills becoming floppy while drying, **place a thin layer of scrunched clingfilm under the frill** until it has dried. Just remember to remove it!

"To prevent sugar paste frills becoming floppy place a thin layer of scrunched clingfilm under the frill."

31.

To prevent any loose crumbs from sticking to your icing or marzipan – coat the cake with either jam or buttercream first.

"To prevent any loose crumbs from sticking to your icing..."

32. **Brush marzipan animals and fruits with confectioner's glaze to give them a lovely shine.** Be sure to clean your brush with glaze cleaner afterwards.

"Brush marzipan animals and fruits with confectioner's glaze to give them a lovely shine."

33.

When rolling out sugar paste or marzipan to cover a cake, **use a pair of** specially designed **spacers** to ensure it is rolled to an equal thickness.

"When rolling out sugar paste use a pair of spacers."

34.

Worry no more! **When taking a special event cake to a venue, pack a 'first aid kit'** of filled piping bag and sugar flowers, in case of emergency repairs.

"When taking a special event cake to a venue, pack a 'first aid kit'.

35.

When working with a dark coloured sugar paste, lightly grease the work surface with white vegetable fat instead of icing sugar to prevent sticking. If you use icing sugar, white flecks could appear on the dark surface and will be almost impossible to remove.

"When working with a dark coloured sugar paste, lightly grease the work surface with white vegetable fat."

36.

Madeira cake is the most suitable for cutting into different shapes as it is less likely to crumble. Or, if using a different type of sponge, freeze and cut into shape while it is still semi-frozen.

"Madeira cake is the most suitable for cutting into different shapes."

37.

If your cake isn't as uniform as you would like, **use buttercream to fill any holes or cracks** and place the cake in the fridge for a couple of hours to set before icing.

"Use buttercream to fill any holes or cracks."

38.

If you are daunted by the thought of painting directly onto a cake surface, **try painting your design onto a sugar paste plaque** instead, that way if you go wrong you can always start again. Plaques can also be made well ahead of time.

"Try painting your design onto a sugar paste plaque."

39.

To prevent your hand wobbling when piping onto a cake, support the icing bag with the fingers of your opposite hand and **keep your elbow close** to your body.

"To prevent your hand wobbling when piping keep your elbow close."

40.

When attempting to pipe a straight line, always **pipe towards yourself,** not away.

"Pipe towards yourself."

41.

When royal icing appears too soft, always try beating it first before attempting to thicken it with more sugar. The beating alone may well stiffen it sufficiently, but adding too much sugar could make it too heavy.

"When royal icing appears too soft, always try beating it first.

42.

To achieve a soft sheen on your sugar paste icing, gently polish it with the palm of your hand, or better still, a special cake smoother.

"To achieve a soft sheen on your sugar paste icing, gently polish it.

43.

A simple way to decorate a cake covered with buttercream **is to sieve a light coating of cocoa powder over the surface,** and then, using the blade of a knife, draw across the cake in lines to form a feather effect.

"A simple way to decorate a cake is to sieve a light coating of cocoa powder over the surface."

44.

Just before icing a cake already covered with marzipan, **brush the surface with a little clear alcohol,** such as gin or vodka, **to prevent any bacteria forming** between the layers.

"Brush the surface with a little clear alcohol, to prevent any bacteria forming."

45.

If cracks have appeared in your sugar paste icing and it is still soft, rub gently with your hand, or, if need be, wait a day to let it dry and **fill with a small amount of paste** softened with water.

"If cracks have appeared in your sugar paste icing fill with a small amount of paste."

46.

Left-handed decorators do not despair – some suppliers sell petal tubes especially for left-handed people.

"Left-handed decorators do not despair.

47. When making sugar paste models, **use a cutting wheel to shape the paste instead of a knife** as it won't drag and distort the paste.

"**Use a cutting wheel to shape the paste instead of a knife.** "

48.

Always **use chocolate plastique** rather than ganache **to cover a multi-tiered cake** as it is more stable.

"Use chocolate plastique to cover a multi-tiered cake."

49.

To make tiny chocolate curls the easy way, use a potato peeler to shave the curls off the side of a block of chocolate.

"To make tiny chocolate curls the easy way, use a potato peeler."

50. **To colour white chocolate, use powdered food colouring.** Liquid colouring will cause the chocolate to thicken and become unusable.

"To colour white chocolate, use powdered food colouring. "

Meg Boas

After working in food publishing for many years, Meg Boas started her own bespoke wedding and celebration cake business, Lemon Sky Cakes, which she successfully ran for a number of years in Bath. She has now returned to publishing as Commissioning Editor for Absolute Press.

"Meg Boas started her own bespoke wedding and celebration cake business, Lemon Sky Cakes."

**Little Books of Tips from
Absolute Press**

Aga	Gardening
Allotment	Gin
Avocado	Golf
Beer	Herbs
Cake Decorating	Spice
Cheese	Tea
Coffee	Whisky
Fishing	Wine

If you enjoyed this book, try...

THE LITTLE BOOK OF

TEA

TIPS

"Keep stored tea well away from strong smelling foods."

"Buy loose tea leaves rather than tea bags."

ABSOLUTE PRESS

An imprint of Bloomsbury Publishing Plc

50 Bedford Square	1385 Broadway
London	New York
WC1B 3DP	NY 10018
UK	USA

www.bloomsbury.com

ABSOLUTE PRESS and the A. logo are trademarks of Bloomsbury Publishing Plc

First published in 2008
This edition printed 2018

A catalogue record for this book is available from the British Library.
Library of Congress Cataloguing-in-Publication data has been applied for.
ISBN 13: 9781472954657

Printed and bound in Spain by Tallers Grafics Soler